W9-BJN-519

DATE DUE

GAYLORD			PRINTED IN U.S.A.

TURKEYS

BARNYARD FRIENDS

Jason Cooper

The Rourke Book Co., Inc.
Vero Beach, Florida 32964

Edited by Sandra A. Robinson and Pamela J.P. Schroeder

PHOTO CREDITS
All photos © Lynn M. Stone

Library of Congress Cataloging-in-Publication Data

Cooper, Jason, 1942-
    Turkeys / by Jason Cooper.
    p. cm. — (Barn yard friends)
    Includes index.
    ISBN 1-55916-092-6
    1. Turkeys—Juvenile literature. [1. Turkeys. 2. Farm life.]
I. Title. II. Series: Cooper, Jason, 1942- Barn yard friends.
SF507.C65   1995
636.5'92—dc20
                                          94-39537
                                               CIP
                                               AC

Printed in the USA

TABLE OF CONTENTS

TURKEYS

Turkey is the favorite Thanksgiving dish of Americans and Canadians. Turkeys are also the only birds of the barnyard that came from North America.

Domestic, or tame, turkeys were first raised from wild turkeys in the United States, Canada and Mexico. Other kinds of **poultry** — domestic ducks, geese and chickens — were raised from their wild cousins in Europe and Asia.

Native Americans raised the first tame turkeys hundreds of years ago. Today, farmers raise millions of turkeys.

Wild turkeys like these are the ancestors of today's domestic turkeys

HOW TURKEYS LOOK

Turkeys are the largest barnyard birds. A tom, or male, turkey can weigh 50 pounds!

A tom turkey shows off by strutting and raising its long tail feathers like a fan. The tom hopes to attract a female turkey with his show.

Turkeys are related to chickens and pheasants. Like them, turkeys have bare legs, long toes, and a short, sharp bill.

Most domestic turkeys are white, but they have featherless, red necks. They also have a long, stringlike "beard" on their breast.

An old tom turkey (left) wears a long, stringlike "beard"

WHERE TURKEYS LIVE

Farmers keep young turkeys in barns. After the turkeys are about six weeks old, they are free to wander around an outdoor pen. They can return indoors to escape bad weather.

Hen, or female, turkeys need different kinds and amounts of food than toms. Farmers separate hens and toms so that they can feed each group what they need.

Turkey farms are scattered throughout North America. North Carolina produces the most adult turkeys.

Young tom turkeys grow up in an outdoor pen

BREEDS OF TURKEYS

Turkeys all belong to one **breed,** or basic kind. However, by carefully choosing which turkeys to use as mothers and fathers, turkey farmers have raised several **varieties.** Each variety is a different color, size or both.

Today, nearly all turkeys belong to the white Holland variety. Seven other varieties, including six with dark feathers, are quite rare.

This domestic bronze turkey looks a lot like a wild turkey

Often called "gobblers" because of their gobble call, male turkeys wear
bright, fleshy wattles over their bill

With frost on the grass by this turkey pen, Thanksgiving cannot be too far away

WILD TURKEYS

Wild turkeys live in almost every U.S. state, and in northern Mexico and southern Canada. Wild turkeys live in flocks. They feed on acorns, berries and insects.

Wild turkeys rarely weigh more than 15 pounds. They have stronger legs and wings than domestic turkeys. Wild turkeys like to run away from danger, but they can fly well for short distances if they have to.

Wild turkeys roost in trees, where they are safe from most animals that would attack

BABY TURKEYS

Some farmers keep turkeys just to lay eggs. These "egg farms" are called **hatcheries.** As soon as the eggs hatch, the **poults,** or babies, are sold to farmers who raise the young turkeys.

Poults take about five months to become adults. Turkeys can live for several years. However, they are usually butchered — killed for their meat — when they are five months old.

Turkey poults, huddled together, help each other keep warm

HOW TURKEYS ARE RAISED

Farmers keep baby turkeys indoors. Poults huddle together in the turkey shed under heaters to keep warm. Farmers keep the turkey sheds warm until the poults are about six weeks old. Then the turkeys go outdoors.

Farmers feed turkeys corn, soybean oil meal and other healthy foods. Turkeys also pick up some wild food from the ground in their pens.

These baby turkeys eat from trays (upper left) and warm themselves under domed heaters (top)

HOW TURKEYS ACT

Wild turkeys are very alert, so they are difficult for hunters to shoot. Domestic turkeys, though, are used to people. They show little or no fear. Sometimes, like curious kittens, they walk up to people who visit their pens.

Domestic turkeys peck at each other in their pens, just as chickens and pheasants will. Farmers clip part of the turkey's bill when it hatches. That prevents turkeys from hurting each other.

Squabbles are common in flocks of domestic turkeys

HOW TURKEYS ARE USED

Turkeys are an important source of food in North America. Each American eats an average of 15 pounds of turkey each year.

Most of a domestic turkey's body can be used for meat. However, almost every part of a turkey is useful. A turkey's insides are cooked, ground up and used in animal foods. Turkey feathers are ground up for use as farm fertilizer — and turkey feed.

Glossary

breed (BREED) — a special group or type of an animal, such as a *white Holland* turkey

domestic (dum ES tihk) — referring to any of several kinds of animals tamed and raised by humans

hatchery (HATCH er ree) — a place where large numbers of eggs are produced

hen (HEN) — a female turkey

poult (POLT) — a young turkey

poultry (POLE tree) — domestic birds, especially chickens, turkeys and ducks

variety (var I eh tee) — a group of animals that is slightly different from other groups of the same kind of animal, such as a *bronze* turkey